THIS BOOK BELONGS TO:

Lumi the Light
Learns to Shine

Kelley Tsika

DESTINY IMAGE® PUBLISHERS, INC.
P.O. Box 310, Shippensburg, PA 17257-0310
"Promoting Inspired Lives"

Illustrations by Natalia Hubbert
www.NataliaHubbert.com

Author photo by Shelby Tsika
shelbytsikaphotography.com

This book and all other Destiny Image and Destiny Image Fiction books are available at Christian bookstores and distributors worldwide.

For more information on foreign distributors, call 717-532-3040.
Or reach us on the Internet: www.destinyimage.com

ISBN HC: 978-0-7684-5056-9
ISBN Ebook: 978-0-7684-5057-6

For Worldwide Distribution, Printed in the U.S.A.
1 2 3 4 5 6 /24 23 22 21 20 19

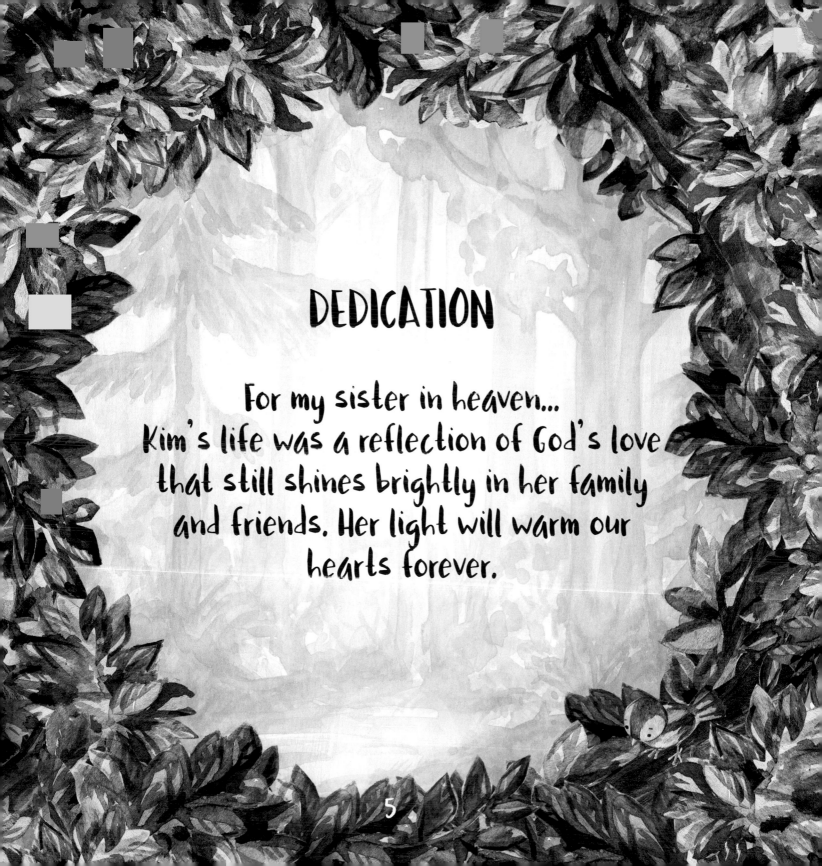

DEDICATION

For my sister in heaven...
Kim's life was a reflection of God's love
that still shines brightly in her family
and friends. Her light will warm our
hearts forever.

PREFACE

Lumi the Light Learns to Shine is a story that echoes my heart. My hope for this book is to help little ones realize their potential early in life. God has given each of His children wonderfully unique gifts and abilities. He does not want us to hide these away.

Sometimes we let fear come in, disable us, and keep us hidden away from the potential God has given us. We miss blessing after blessing hiding our light. My prayer is that each set of hands this book falls into will be given freedom from that fear and encouragement to let their light and God-given gifts shine out into the world.

One gray and cloudy day, Lumi the Light felt afraid.

She searched for a hiding place. Somewhere to help her feel safe and secure.

10

Lumi floated from place to place until she found a big, beautiful tree in a thick, green forest.

"I'll be safe here," she thought to herself.
"Nothing will harm me or darken my light under this tree!"

Lumi felt alright for a while but in her heart she knew she was incomplete.
Under that tree, she was not really living the life she was meant to live.

Suddenly, she heard rustling leaves and groaning.

When she looked through the thick leaves of her tree, she saw a traveler having a hard time making his way through the dark forest.

He eventually fell down with a loud THUD right in front of Lumi and her tree!

16

The traveler noticed a small glimmer in the darkness. Lumi decided to move in closer. "What is the matter? Why did you fall?" Lumi asked him.

Lumi suddenly knew she was faced with a very important decision. Stay safe under her tree or leave her tree, light the way, and help this needy person.

19

Lumi felt the presence of her Heavenly Father and Creator. These verses came to her.

You are the light of the world. A city that is set on a hill and cannot be hidden. Nor do they light a candle and put it under a bush, but on a candlestick, and it gives light to all who are in the house. Let your light so shine before men, that they may see your good works glorify your Father in heaven. (Matthew 5:14-16)

The word of God filled her heart and she knew what to do.
She jumped out from under that tree onto the traveler's
walking stick, that felt very much like a candlestick,
and decided to do what she does best, SHINE!

She helped the traveler get safely through the dark forest that night and he was very thankful.

Lumi helped someone that needed her and shone much brighter than she ever would if she had stayed under that big tree.

23

From that moment on, Lumi the Light was happy knowing she was finally living the life God created her for.

The End.

25

Think About It ...
(discussion time)

Lumi is a bright and shiny light, yet she is scared to shine her light. Why do you think she's scared?

Have you ever been scared? If so, it's ok! What are some ways that will help you not feel so scared?

What do you think would have happened to the traveler if Lumi had stayed hidden away?

What would have happened to Lumi if she had made a different choice?

God says to love our neighbors as ourselves (Matthew 22: 38-39).
The traveler was Lumi's neighbor that day.
Who is your "neighbor" and how can you help?

ABOUT THE AUTHOR

Kelley Tsika has worked with children her whole life. From babysitting in her younger years, working with youth in schools and church settings to getting her bachelor's degree in family science and child development and going on to work in children's hospitals in a professional capacity as a Child Life Specialist. Kelley has been married to Thomas Tsika for 28+ years and has 3 children. She has also been involved in Paul E. Tsika Ministries at Restoration Ranch for 15 years. It is her hope to encourage all children to face their fears, put them in God's hands, and live life to their fullest potential.

PAUL E. TSIKA MINISTRIES INC.

P.O. Box 136
Midfield, Texas 77458
www.plowon.org